Good News!

written by Beth Neuberger

illustrated by Benton Mahan

©1984. The STANDARD PUBLISHING Company, Cincinnati, Ohio
Division of STANDEX INTERNATIONAL Corporation. Printed in U.S.A.
The distinctive trade dress of this book is proprietary to Western Publishing Company, Inc., used with permission.

My name is Peter and I know some good news.

My mom and dad shared this good news with me at breakfast.

And then Dad said, "Peter, we want you to tell our good news to someone else today."

So I thought and thought.

"Rusty, I will tell our good news to Mr. King, the mailman." Rusty wagged his tail. He thought telling Mr. King was a very good idea.

I waited on the step for the mailman to come. "Mr. King, I've got some good news for you!"

Mr. King listened to my good news. Then he smiled. "Peter, I will tell this good news to someone on my mail route."

Mr. King walked down the block. He gave Mrs. Lee three letters and he shared the good news with her.

Mrs. Lee liked what Mr. King said. She waved to her paperboy. "Mark, come have a cookie. I want to tell you some good news."

Mark grinned when he heard the good news. He jumped on his bike and pedaled to the library. Mr. Jones sat behind a big desk. Mark stood on his tiptoes and whispered, "I know something super!"

At noon Mr. Jones crossed the street to a tall office building. He looked up. Mr. Bell was washing windows high above the sidewalk. Mr. Jones shouted the good news up to him.

After work Mr. Bell went home. "Mary, I heard some good news today." He told his wife the good news and she hugged him. Then Mrs. Bell shared the good news with Pam, the babysitter.

Pam went home and told her sister Jill the good news. "Oh, Pam," said Jill, "that good news makes me feel all warm inside!"

The next day Jill ran to school. "Teacher, Teacher, listen to my good news!"

Jill's teacher reported the good news to Mrs. Clark, the principal. "Thank you," said Mrs. Clark. "That is good news!"

Later Mrs. Clark shared the good news with Mr. Green, the crossing guard.

When the ice-cream man came by, Mr. Green said, "I will have a cherry cone." Then he told the ice-cream man the good news. The ice-cream man rang the bell on his truck and drove down the street.

The ice-cream man stopped at the house of my best friend. "Mike," he said, "do I have some good news for you!" He told Mike the good news.

And of course, Mike shared the good news with me.

Now all of us want you to know this good news, too.

It is very simple.

And that is such good news.

Now won't *you* go and tell the good news to someone?